monster
Chronicles

WATCHERS IN THE WOODS

STEPHEN KRENSKY

Lerner Publications Company · Minneapolis

Lerner Publications Company
A division of Lerner Publishing Group, Inc.
241 First Avenue North
Minneapolis, MN 55401

Website address: www.lernerbooks.com

Library of Congress Cataloging-in-Publication Data

Krensky, Stephen.
    Watchers in the woods / by Stephen Krensky.
        p.   cm. — (Monster chronicles)
    Includes bibliographical references and index.
    ISBN 978-0-8225-6763-9 (lib. bdg. : alk. paper)
    1. Dwarfs. 2. Trolls. 3. Elves. 4. Goblins. I. Title.
    GR555.K74 2008
    599.9'49—dc22   2006101873

Manufactured in the United States of America
1 2 3 4 5 6 - JR - 13 12 11 10 09 08

TABLE OF CONTENTS

1 WHO'S REALLY OUT THERE?

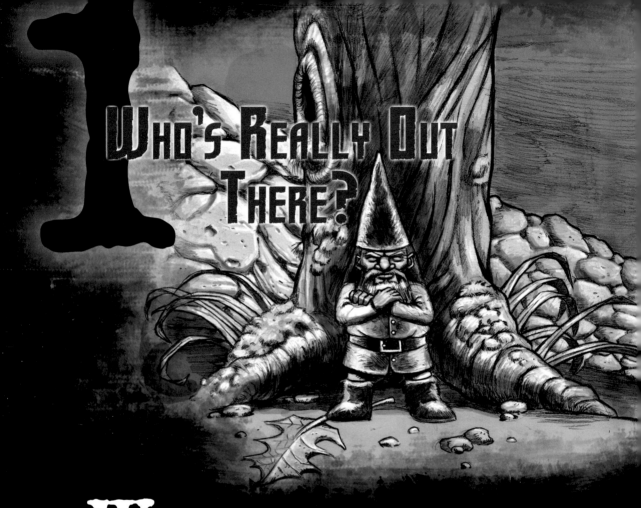

When you think of the woods, you probably think of trees. You may think of birds, deer, and maybe the occasional bear. To many modern people, the woods are someplace to go on a nature walk. But this wasn't always so. Long ago,

many people lived close to the woods, in villages and on farms at the edges of enormous forests.

These people were familiar enough with the woods. They used forest timber to build their houses. They gathered firewood, mushrooms, and herbs in among the tall trees. They cut paths through the forests from one town to another.

But the woods could also be dark and mysterious places. They were filled with noises, not all of which people could identify. Walking through the forest, you might hear a rustle in the leaves and then see a blur of motion. Was that an animal or something else? And sometimes at night, mysterious lights appeared and disappeared among the trees. There seemed to be a whole world of activity contained in the forest and people weren't convinced it was all birds and deer.

People peered into the deep shadows of the forest and wondered, "Are there creatures in there we don't know about—hiding behind rocks or inside tree trunks or under bridges?" And then they wondered, "We can't see them, but can they see us? Are they *watching* us?"

So what—or who—did people think these watchers in the woods were? There are many old stories about them. Europe, for example, was (and still is, in some places) home to many forests. No surprise then that European folklore has many kinds of watchers in various shapes and sizes. There are trolls, goblins, dwarfs, and gnomes to name a few.

The dark, dense forests of Europe led many people to tell tales of trolls, goblins, dwarfs, and gnomes that they thought could be found there.

Some European watchers have different names in different places. Germany has dwarfs, but it also has *erdleute* and *stillevolk*. Scandinavia has trolls and *hulderfolk*. The Irish have their leprechauns and the

Dwarfs have different names in different regions of the world. In central Africa, dwarfs are known as *biloko*, while in Mexico they are called *chanques*. Eastern Europeans call dwarfs *karliki*.

Scots their boggarts. But all these watchers have something in common—they are the mysterious folk who live just beyond the edge of the human world.

WHERE DO WATCHERS COME FROM?

There are many legends about the origins of watchers. One legend comes from the story of Adam and Eve, the first man and woman created by God in Jewish and Christian tradition. After they left the Garden of Eden, Adam and Eve and their children lived as farmers. Although the story isn't in the Bible, legend claims that God one day stopped by Adam and Eve's home for a visit. Eve had not been expecting company, and she was a little embarrassed. Only two of her children—a boy and a girl—were properly cleaned up and fit to be seen. Her other children

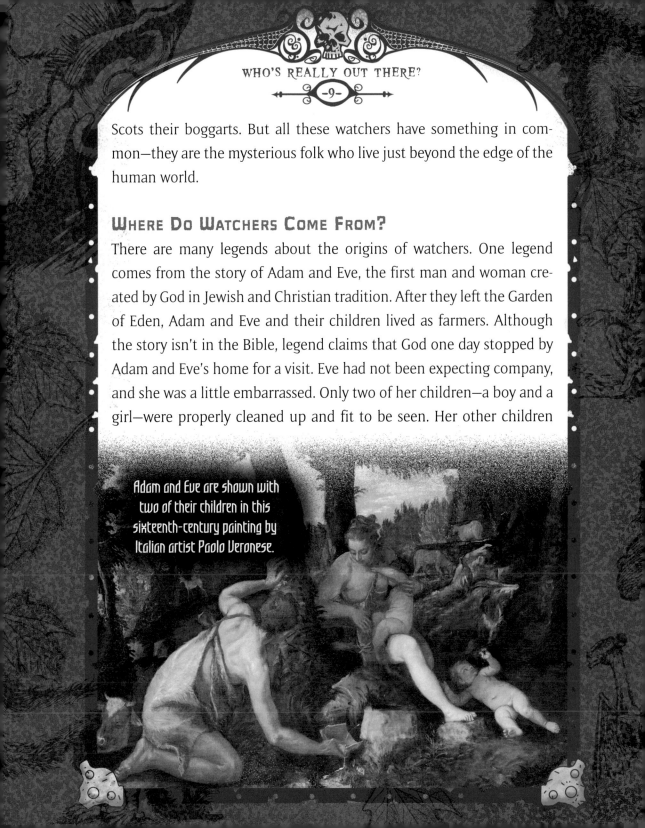

Adam and Eve are shown with two of their children in this sixteenth-century painting by Italian artist Paolo Veronese.

were dirty and poorly dressed. So Eve kept them hidden away. When God asked to see her children, Eve only brought out the boy and the girl. "Where are your other children?" God asked. "All my children stand before you," Eve insisted.

What was she thinking? This was God she was talking to, the one who sees all and knows all. But Eve was nervous and spoke without thinking. Sadly, her other children paid a high price for her error. God told Eve that since she had kept these children hidden away, they would remain hidden for all time. They would grow no taller than they had grown already. They would stay the size of children their whole lives.

However, God gave the hidden children many powers. They could change their shape or make themselves invisible. Some could grant wishes or live for hundreds of years. And some possessed great skill with gold and silver and jewels and could make them into many beautiful things.

Another explanation comes from the Eddas, a collection of tales from Iceland. The Eddas themselves are based on Scandinavian lore—myths and folklore from Sweden, Norway, Denmark, and Finland. In the Eddas, the first gods killed a giant named Ymir. Ymir was so large that

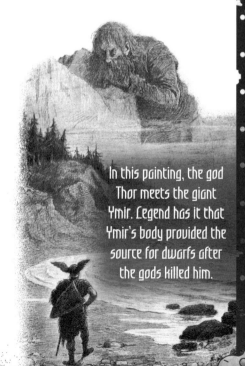

In this painting, the god Thor meets the giant Ymir. Legend has it that Ymir's body provided the source for dwarfs after the gods killed him.

his body provided the materials to make the earth and the seas. His decaying body was also the source of dwarfs, who popped out of him like sprouts in the early spring. The gods taught the dwarfs to speak and helped shape them into figures with arms and legs. The dwarfs then made good use of their limbs. They mined the metal from caves under the forest and fashioned it into swords, shields, and jewelry.

OTHER TALES

The mythology of ancient Ireland, Scotland, and Wales tells yet another tale of the origins of some watchers. According to myth, when some of the ancient gods lost a battle against an invading race, they went to live in underground mounds. That underground world, the fairy realm, was filled with creatures. Beings such as leprechauns, boggarts, pookas, grogochs, and the tylweth teg lived both in the fairy world and the natural world. The fairy creatures kept an eye on humans to make sure they didn't disturb the natural order of things.

Like dwarfs, Irish leprechauns have jobs. They are shoemakers. They are also said to be very rich and bury their gold to keep it safe. In some stories, if a human catches a leprechaun, the leprechaun must take the person to where the gold is buried. But leprechauns are very good at escaping. If the person takes his eyes off the leprechaun for even a second, the leprechaun disappears. And so does the person's hope of ever finding the buried treasure!

And humans did their best not to provoke the fairies' fierce tempers.

As explorers and seafarers settled in different parts of Europe and the

British Isles, they took their folk tales with them. Their tales mingled with local stories to create much lore about the watchers in the woods. Adding to this old lore, other stories of trolls, goblins, fairies, and the like sprang up anywhere that unexplained noises or unexplained shapes passed in the night.

WHERE ARE THE WATCHERS NOW?

Watchers and people once had a pretty workable understanding of each other. Watchers had their place, and humans had theirs. But eventually, humans felt a need for growth and change. People were always in a hurry to improve their lives, to make progress. They built bigger villages, then towns, then cities. On the other hand, stories about watchers say they were pretty satisfied with a simple existence and were in no hurry to change it. So watchers stopped living openly among human beings. Over time, the watchers grew to mistrust humans.

In tales, watchers still spent some time out in the open. But many of them began to live underground. Some are said to inhabit natural caves while others build homes in caverns and tunnels. Some of these dwellings are connected in a kind of underground town.

In stories, watchers do a lot of digging in the earth. So it's only natural that they have found so much gold over the centuries. They are quite drawn to it. Watchers have to stay away from the sun and daylight (to avoid humans), so they enjoy the gleam of gold instead.

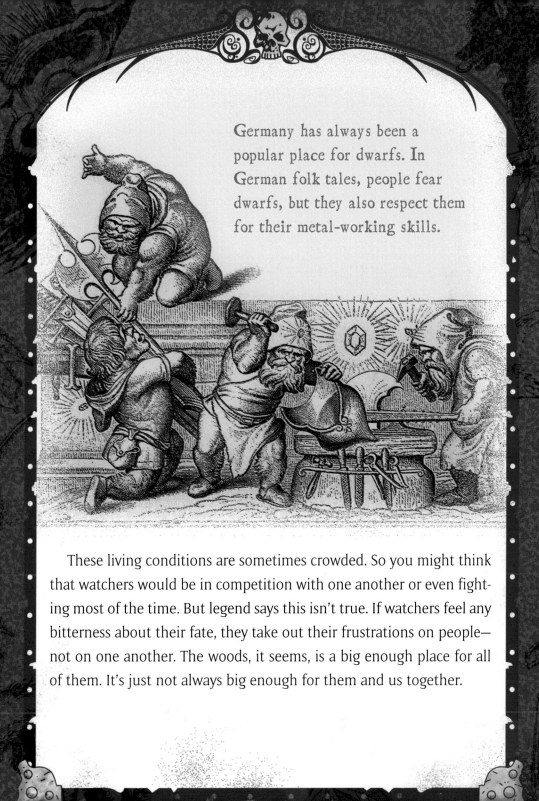

Germany has always been a popular place for dwarfs. In German folk tales, people fear dwarfs, but they also respect them for their metal-working skills.

These living conditions are sometimes crowded. So you might think that watchers would be in competition with one another or even fighting most of the time. But legend says this isn't true. If watchers feel any bitterness about their fate, they take out their frustrations on people—not on one another. The woods, it seems, is a big enough place for all of them. It's just not always big enough for them and us together.

2 Dwarfs and Goblins and Trolls—Oh, My!

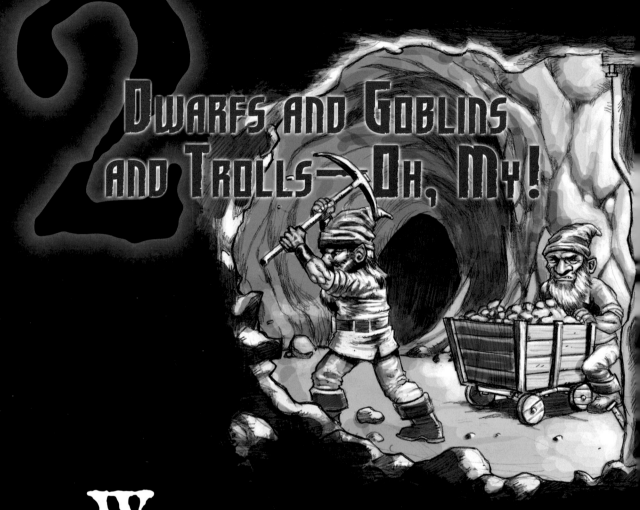

With so many watchers, it can be hard sometimes to tell them apart. They share certain traits from our point of view. They have exaggerated noses, eyes, and ears. Watchers may have hair growing out of unexpected places, such as

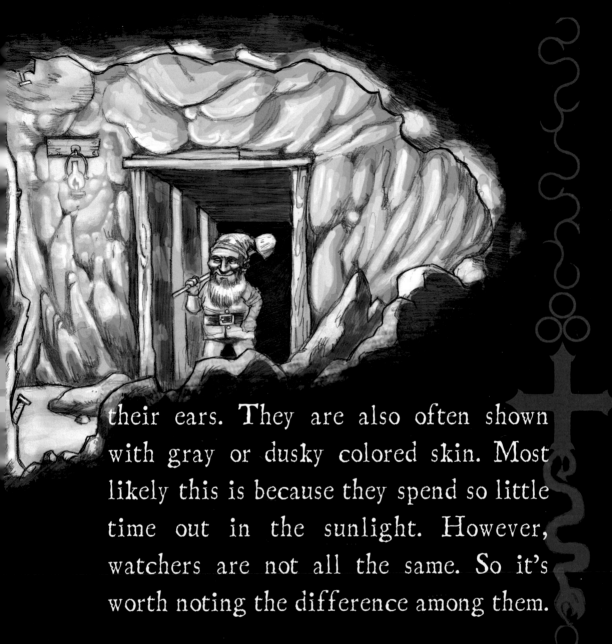

their ears. They are also often shown with gray or dusky colored skin. Most likely this is because they spend so little time out in the sunlight. However, watchers are not all the same. So it's worth noting the difference among them.

DWARFS

Dwarfs are probably the hardest working watchers in legend. They are famous as miners and smiths, working with hot metals to shape them into useful and beautiful objects. Dwarfs are much stronger than you'd

According to legend, dwarfs find great jewels and precious metals in the earth, as shown in this English illustration from 1893. But some dwarfs also have the power to turn coal into diamonds and straw into gold.

think, given their small size. And their enormous energy enables them to work for hours on end.

Dwarfs are sometimes described as looking like stones or boulders heaped together into a short compact pile. Although they are the same height as human children, they are much broader. The men are often bearded.

Mostly, tales say that dwarfs like to be left alone. But if they perform a kindness for a peasant or a whole village, they like to be thanked. Dwarfs can get prickly when they think they have been insulted. If you don't thank them properly, you may find your cow giving sour milk or your hens laying eggs of stone.

Scottish folklore is filled with tales of brownies, a type of elf. Brownies are usually pleasant and helpful to humans. But if offended, a brownie can turn into a boggart, a hostile mischief-maker that's more like a goblin.

GOBLINS

Goblins got their start in French folklore, but they quickly made their way across the rest of western Europe. They are said to live in hollow tree trunks, under the roots of trees, and in large cracks in rocky hillsides. Venturing out from these homes, goblins mostly roam the countryside causing mischief.

Goblins are a little taller than dwarfs, with long limbs, big noses and ears, and warts and other bumps sticking out here and there. It would be nice to say something positive about these creatures, but that isn't easy. Goblins don't work hard or make useful things. It is said that a goblin's smile makes blood curdle, and his laugh turns milk sour. About the best you can say is that some goblins are less bad than others. The more harmless ones just bang on the walls of houses and sneak inside to break dishes when no one is looking.

Nastier goblins are known for playing tricks on people. They are said to be able to weave a nightmare and stick it in your ear while you sleep. Another favorite prank is to remove a horse from a barn during the night, ride it for hours, and return it to the barn at dawn. The exhausted horse is then too tired to do any work the next day.

This illustration of goblins is titled "It Is Time." It was published in 1799 as part of *Caprichos*, a collection of artwork by Francisco José de Goya.

The most unpleasant goblin habit in lore is stealing human babies. European Christians believed that a baby who hadn't been baptized was at great risk of being snatched by goblins. Anxious parents protected their infants by placing a piece of iron or bread near the cradle. Both were thought to be effective protection, since goblin intruders won't go near either. According to folklore, when a

Hobgoblins (*above*) are a sort of kinder, gentler goblin. Hobgoblins are said to play practical jokes on people but don't do anything really mean or harmful.

goblin steals a human child, it leaves one of its own babies behind in the cradle. This only makes the deed doubly evil, because the goblins are deserting their own children while stealing someone else's.

TROLLS

Trolls, like this one from a Norse folktale (*above*), only live in northern climates. Living in a warm and sunny place might make them happy, and they don't want to take any chances. Trolls just aren't meant to be happy.

Stories about trolls come to us from Scandinavian lore. Among all the other pint-sized watchers, trolls are an exception. They are usually big—often eight or nine feet tall. And they are amazingly strong. Some trolls have the strength of ten or twenty men. And if two heads are better than one, some trolls are really lucky—they can have as many as twelve heads. But no matter how many heads they have, trolls are not very smart. Luckily, too, they turn to stone in the sunlight. If not for these handicaps, they might have long ago overrun the houses of men.

Staying neat and clean are not troll virtues. They grow hair in all kinds of places and pretty much never cut it. Some trolls are so shaggy that their hair is filled with burrs and twigs. (The occasional brave bird sometimes even builds a nest in it.) The hair in their ears is actually helpful because trolls supposedly have a great dislike for noise, and the hair helps block it out.

In tales, trolls usually live in caves. Given their bad tempers, trolls often live alone. But they like to keep pets, such as cats. Troll cats are as big as raccoons. Trolls also have their own roosters that crow at the end of the day. The rooster's cock-a-doodle-doo tells the trolls it is safe to come out because the sun has gone down.

When storybook characters hear trolls talking in the distance, their voices rumble like thunder. But if trolls are nearby, the sound of their voices isn't the biggest problem. A person should be much more worried about getting caught by one, for trolls are known to eat people. Trolls prefer to cook people before eating them, but they are not always that fussy.

Elves are another type of watcher from German folklore. Elves are said to be very beautiful creatures that live in the forest. Some elves are tiny, while others are the size of humans. Elves are so beautiful that they can enchant humans who wander into the forest. Some elves seem to enjoy just teasing humans—tangling their hair, tripping them, or causing bad dreams.

GNOMES

Gnomes were particularly popular in German folklore and fairy tales, but you can find stories about them all over Europe. They are basically miniature trolls. You could hold a gnome in the palm of your hand—that is, if you could ever catch one. Gnomes are said to live for hundreds and hundreds of years. But even with all that time to spend, they don't have much patience. They are known to cause mischief, though they are not deadly like some of their legendary troll cousins.

GNOMES AT HOME

In the 1800s, gnomes became popular garden accessories. Small gnome statues, with brightly painted clothes and pointy hats, appeared in gardens from Germany to the United States. Garden gnomes remain popular. In the late 1970s, U.S. publisher Harry Abrams printed *Gnomes* (*right*), an English-language version of a Dutch book. Filled with illustrations, the book took a humorous look at gnomes and launched a gnome craze. And in 2004, the Roaming Gnome became the face of Travelocity (an online travel agency) in a series of popular TV ads.

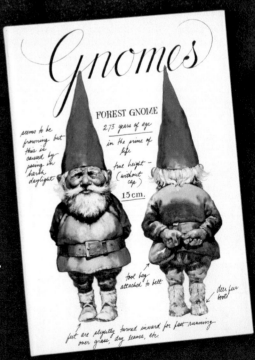

Gnomes

FOREST GNOME
275 years of age
in the prime of life
true height — (without cap)
15 cm.

seems to be frowning but this is caused by passing in harsh daylight

tool bag attached to belt

deer fur boots

feet are slightly turned inward for fast running over grass, dry leaves, etc.

Although many gnomes live in the woods, their small size gives them other options. Some gnomes live on farms in the corners of old barns. They are said to like animals, and so they may choose to live with a human's household pet. But wherever they live, they make themselves right at home. And if you stumble on one, you're better off pretending you didn't see anything. Gnomes like their privacy and their peace and quiet. If disturbed, stories claim that gnomes—like many watchers—will disturb you right back.

This illustration by Francis G. Attwood for the 1895 book *The Fairies Festival* shows the friendly relationship between a gnome and a house cat.

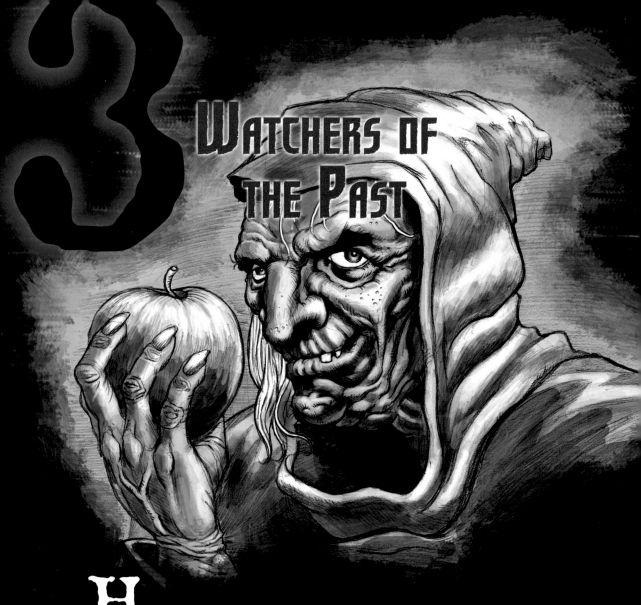

3 Watchers of the Past

Humans seem to love to tell stories about watchers. But watchers are said to be sensitive about how they're portrayed in those stories. They object to tales where they're the bad guy or where they are made to look foolish. Watchers think well of themselves, and they prefer to look back on the great feats of their ancestors.

WHEN DWARFS ARE THE GOOD GUYS

Scandinavian watchers are said to be particularly proud of four dwarfs from Norse mythology. Two of those dwarfs are famous for helping Loki, the god of mischief, after he ran afoul of Thor, the god of thunder. As a joke, Loki cut off the beautiful golden hair of Sif, Thor's wife. Since Thor was big, strong, and bad-tempered, this was not the smartest thing Loki could

In Norse myth, the dwarfs made a great warship, *Skidbladnir*, for the gods. It was big enough to hold all the gods, and yet it could be folded up and carried when not needed.

have done. But Loki was lucky enough to convince the two dwarfs to spin gold into threads so fine that Sif could wear them in place of her stolen hair. When Sif put the dwarf-spun gold on her head, it took root and continued to grow.

Two other dwarfs made Thor his mighty hammer, Mjollnir. Mjollnir could break anything it hit, and it would always return to Thor's hand. Thor used Mjollnir many times in battle against the ice giants, the Norse gods' dreaded enemies.

Dwarfs have also played the hero in other later tales. Famously, they appear in a story about Snow White, a character from German fairy tales. In the early 1800s, two

This illustration by American artist Katharine Pyle from her 1930 book *Tales from Norse Mythology* shows mischievous Loki cutting off the hair of Sif, Thor's wife. Loki didn't get into too much trouble though. He convinced dwarfs to spin gold threads to replace Sif's hair.

German professors, Jacob and Wilhelm Grimm, published a Snow White story as part of a collection of traditional stories for children.

The Grimm brothers' tale concerns an evil queen who is jealous of her beautiful stepdaughter, Snow White. The queen orders a huntsman to take Snow White out into the woods and kill her. But the huntsman cannot bring himself to do the evil deed. Instead, he leaves Snow White in the

forest. Alone and afraid, Snow White wanders the woods until she finds a small cottage. No one is home, so she lets herself in and falls asleep on a little bed. Soon, the house's owners—seven dwarfs—return from their work in the mines. At first they are upset to find someone in their home. But soon they are charmed by Snow White. When she tells them the story of her wicked stepmother, they invite her to stay with them.

The story would have ended happily there if not for the evil queen. While looking in her magic mirror, the queen demands to know who is the fairest woman in the land. When the mirror answers, "Snow White,"

This illustration, from the Grimm brothers collection of German fairy tales published in 1812, shows Snow White falling asleep in a dwarf's bed at their cottage in the woods.

The dwarfs mourn Snow White in her crystal coffin after the queen tricks Snow White into eating a poisoned apple. This 1923 illustration is by Austrian artist Marianne Stokes.

the queen realizes that her stepdaughter is still alive. She finds out where Snow White is living. Disguising herself as an old woman, she visits Snow White while the dwarfs are at work. The queen tries twice to kill the girl. But twice the dwarfs save Snow White just in time.

The third time the queen disguises herself as a farmer's wife and gives Snow White a beautiful red apple. Snow White bites into the apple, not knowing that it's poisoned. A piece of the apple lodges in her throat, and she falls down dead. When the dwarfs return, they find her. They cannot bring themselves to bury their beloved friend, so they place her in a crystal coffin, where she lies as beautiful as ever.

One day, a prince is riding through the forest. He stops at the dwarfs' house, looking for a place to spend the night. He sees Snow White and falls instantly in love. He asks the dwarfs if they will give him the coffin.

At first they refuse. But then seeing how much the prince is in love, the dwarfs let him take the coffin. As the prince's servants carry the coffin away, one stumbles, giving the coffin a shake. The jolt dislodges the piece of poisoned apple in Snow White's throat. She wakes up and falls in love with the prince. They marry, and at their wedding feast, the evil queen gets her just punishment. As for the dwarfs, the Grimm brothers' tale doesn't say what happens to them. But we can assume that Snow White and her prince made sure to thank their little friends.

A GOBLIN TO THE RESCUE

A famous English folk tale, Tom Tit Tot, features a young woman who finds herself involved with a peculiar watcher. There are many versions of the story. But in all of them, a wealthy lord overhears a peasant woman bragging about her daughter. Her daughter, the woman claims, can spin five skeins of flax a day. Flax, a plant fiber, is used to make linen. Until the mid-1800s, people made their own clothes out of homespun thread. They spun the flax into thread on wooden wheels and rolled the thread into skeins. Most young women were skilled spinners. But five skeins a day—that was quite a claim for even the best spinner. The lord was surprised by the mother's boast. The girl was even more surprised, for she knew she could never do such a thing.

The lord decided that he would marry such a hardworking and talented—not to mention beautiful—young woman. But she would have to prove to him that she could spin as much flax as her mother claimed. She must do this every day for a month. And if she failed, the lord would sentence her to death.

On the first night of the trial, the maiden was locked in a tower chamber with her flax and a spinning wheel. She sat crying over her misfortune when suddenly, a goblin appeared. He promised to return each night to supply her with all the spun flax she needed—on one condition. Each night he would give her three chances to guess his name. If she failed to guess correctly by the end of the month, she would have to become his wife.

The girl, facing certain death, was in no position to argue. And so each night the goblin mysteriously appeared. The girl tried to guess his name and failed.

This 1889 illustration is by Henry J. Ford from Andrew Lang's *The Blue Fairy Book*. In it, a goblin appears to the forlorn maiden and offers to help her spin all the flax she needs.

But as promised, the goblin gave her the promised flax. So each morning she had five skeins to give to her lord. He was delighted, of course, to see that she truly possessed such skill. She was less pleased because, try as she might, she had had no luck guessing the goblin's name.

By the end of the month, the girl was very upset, thinking that she would have to marry a goblin. When the lord came in to visit her, he could see that she had been crying. This puzzled him, since clearly she

was almost done with her work. To cheer her up, he told her of something strange he had seen in the forest. It was a goblin sitting at a spinning wheel singing a nonsense song. The song had stuck in the lord's head, and he sang it for the girl. When he got to the part where the goblin spoke his name aloud, the girl smiled.

In the morning the goblin appeared, flax in hand, ready to leave with his new bride. But she still had three guesses left. She wasted the first two, and then pointed at him while reciting the third. "Nimmy, nimmy, not," she said. "Your name is Tom Tit Tot." Well, the goblin was astonished, but there was nothing he could do but vanish forever.

This illustration of the character Rumpelstiltskin appeared in one of the Grimm brothers' books.

If the story sounds familiar, it may be because there's a similar Grimm brothers fairy tale. In that version, a young woman faces the impossible task of spinning straw into gold. She is helped by a mysterious dwarf. As a reward for his aid, the dwarf demands that woman promise him her first-born child. After the woman marries and gives birth, the dwarf returns to collect his reward. But the woman outsmarts him by guessing his magical name: Rumpelstiltskin.

This illustration of "The Three Billy Goats Gruff" tale is from the 1859 book *Popular Tales from the Norse* translated into English by English writer George W. Dasent.

A Very Gruff Encounter

"The Three Billy Goats Gruff" is a Norwegian tale and probably one of the most famous troll stories. But it's not a story that trolls are fond of— and with good reason. The tale begins with three billy goats (that is, male goats) all named Gruff. They were traveling up a hillside and had to cross a cold stream. There was a bridge over the stream, but the bridge was guarded by a fearsome troll.

The youngest billy goat, having scampered ahead, approached the bridge first. The troll jumped out and threatened to eat the goat at once. "Don't waste your time on me," protested the little goat. "The goat coming after me is much bigger and fatter." Not wanting to spoil his appetite on a snack, the troll took the first goat's advice and decided to wait. Pretty soon along came the second billy goat. Again, the troll jumped out and threatened to gobble him up. But the second billy goat told the troll that he would do well to wait for the last goat, which was the biggest and fattest of all. The troll was pleased when the third billy goat Gruff appeared, as this goat was truly big and fat. "I am going to gobble you up," the troll declared.

But the third billy goat wasn't the biggest of the three for nothing. He lowered his horns and charged the troll. The collision sounded like a great clap of thunder. The troll was knocked clear over the water and far away into the woods. The third billy goat then continued on his way. This was a much happier ending for him than it was for the troll.

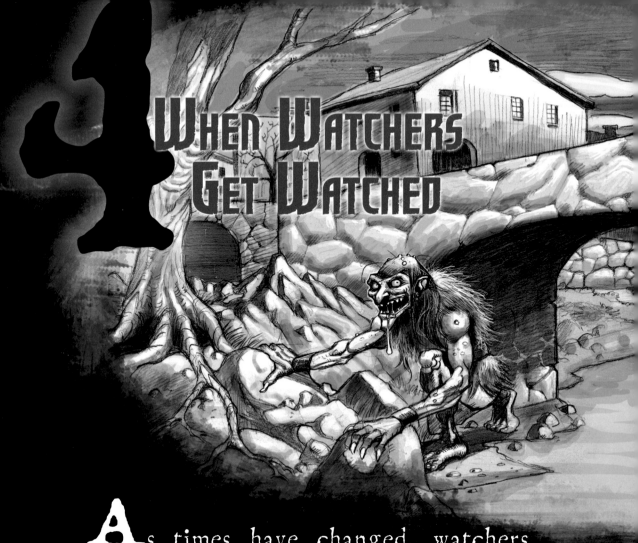

WHEN WATCHERS GET WATCHED

As times have changed, watchers have stubbornly stuck to their old ways. They have shown no interest in modern conveniences or updated technologies. Watchers don't care about computers, televisions, or microwave ovens. They

live as they have always lived, even as the world changes around them. They are also as grumpy as ever, which is clear from the stories still being told about them.

WATCHERS IN PRINT

The Hobbit (1937), a novel by J. R. R. Tolkien, centers on the adventures of Bilbo Baggins, a hobbit (a small humanlike creature). The story of

This illustration from *The Princess and the Goblin* shows Curdie ready to confront the goblins after they break into the king's cellar.

THE PRINCESS AND THE GOBLIN

Goblins are up to their usual evil doings in *The Princess and the Goblin* (1872) by Scottish author George Macdonald. The goblins threaten to kidnap a princess and flood a mine. Standing in the way of their scheme is a young miner, Curdie. Curdie is a practical boy, but if he hopes to succeed in defeating the goblins, he will need to believe in magic.

hobbits doesn't come directly from folklore. Tolkien created the characters. But Tolkien draws on many other folklore watchers to fill his novel, including trolls, goblins, elves, and dwarfs.

As the story begins, Bilbo Baggins is a hobbit living in the land of Middle Earth. Like most hobbits, Bilbo is cheerful but very private. He stays close to home and sticks mostly to his own kind. But when a group of dwarfs invites Bilbo to join them on a quest to reclaim treasure from a fiery dragon, he can hardly refuse. Along the way, Bilbo gets the better of some trolls and finds a mysterious ring deep underground in a goblin cave. (This ring is later revealed to have great power, and it becomes the centerpiece of Tolkien's series of novels known as *The Lord of the Rings.*)

George Macdonald helped Lewis Carroll, the author of *Alice in Wonderland*, with Carroll's early writing efforts. Macdonald was also an inspiration to later fantasy writers J. R. R. Tolkien and C. S. Lewis.

Goblins don't often figure in religious stories, but they do in *Herschel and the Hanukkah Goblins* (1989), a traditional story adapted by Eric Kimmel. The story opens as a young traveler arrives in a town just in time to celebrate the Jewish holiday of Hanukkah. But there will be no celebration, he learns, because a group of goblins is terrorizing

the town. The only way to get rid of them is to light a candle on each night of Hanukkah, something the goblins will try and stop at all costs. No one in town is brave enough to stand up to the goblins. Luckily, Herschel is not only brave, he's also smart, and he manages to outwit them all.

Another young boy faces some interesting creatures in the Harry Potter series of novels (1997–2007) by J. K. Rowling. The title character, Harry, discovers an entire world of magic after he is accepted to the Hogwarts School of Witchcraft and Wizardry. Drawn into this mysterious Hogwarts world, Harry meets goblins, trolls, and the occasional elf.

Some of the goblins in J. K. Rowling's Harry Potter novels have the important responsibility of running Gringotts Bank. That's where all the magical characters keep their money.

MOVIE WATCHERS ON THE LOOSE

Apparently, there's a good reason for watchers to stay in the woods. When they get out, trouble follows. The movie *Gremlins* (1984) features a small furry watcher with big ears and eyes. Called a mogwai, the creature appears sweet and adorable. But if the mogwai is not treated with the proper care, it can turn out to be not so cute. Billy Peltzer (played by Zach Galligan) gets the mogwai as a pet. It comes with three simple rules: no water, no feeding after midnight, and no bright lights. When these rules are broken, the sweet little creature transforms into something nasty. It multiplies, too, and soon Billy and his whole town are overrun with green-skinned gremlins bent on causing havoc.

DWARF-SIZED STATUE

Walt Disney's 1937 *Snow White and the Seven Dwarfs (above)* was
the first full-length animated movie in the United States. It took
hundreds of artists three years to complete. When the film won an
Academy Award in 1939, Walt Disney was presented with one
full-sized and seven dwarf-sized award statues.

Of course, when watchers stay in the woods, they can be trouble too. In the movie *Legend* (1985), a peasant named Jack (Tom Cruise) lives in an enchanted forest with his beloved Lily (Mia Sara). But that peaceful life is disturbed when the evil Lord of Darkness (Tim Curry) sends some marauding trolls to steal the horn of a unicorn. This theft makes the world dark and cold, just the way the Lord of Darkness likes it. Even worse, Lily falls under the spell of the dark forces—where she will remain unless Jack (and a band of elves that he recruits) can save the day.

Saving the day in a smaller way also figures in *Labyrinth* (1986). Here, the old expression "Be careful what you wish for" certainly applies to Sarah (Jennifer Connolly). This teenage girl daydreams about living in a fairy tale world instead of the real one. One day, while she is babysitting her annoying little brother, Toby, she wishes that Jareth the Goblin

Jareth the Goblin King (played by David Bowie) and his goblin friends kidnap a toddler (Toby Froud) in the fantasy movie *Labyrinth* (1986).

King would just take Toby away. To her horror, the wish comes true. Jareth (David Bowie) abducts her brother, and Sarah must rescue him. Along the way, she meets a number of muppet-like creatures while she makes her way through a tricky labyrinth (maze).

While one goblin king is bad, countless ordinary goblins are even worse. There are thousands of these creatures in the movie trilogy based on Tolkien's *Lord of the Ring* novels—*The Fellowship of the Ring* (2002), *The Two Towers* (2003), and *The Return of the King* (2004). Tolkien called these goblin-like creatures orcs. They are evil watchers in every sense imaginable. And the problem for the heroes is that these watchers are not staying in the woods. Under their leaders, Sauron and Saruman, their armies are overrunning the realm of Middle Earth.

The Fellowship, including a dwarf, an elf, and some hobbits, face off against evil orcs *(shown below)* in the first *Lord of the Rings* movie, *The Fellowship of the Ring* (2002).

GREEN GOBLIN

The Green Goblin is one of comic-book-hero Spider-Man's fiercest foes. The goblin first appeared in Marvel comic books in the 1960s. He is also featured in the movies *Spider-Man* (2002, *shown above*) and *Spider-Man 2* (2004). The Green Goblin was not born a goblin. He was a human transformed by an unstable potion.

We can only hope that we will never face the same threat in our own world. Stories about watchers in the woods have been around for thousands of years. And despite the creatures' reputation for crankiness, they've really been pretty patient with us. All of our progress and the march of civilization has taken away much of our fear of dark places in the woods, but who knows? If the watchers ever reach a point where they have finally had enough, humans might face some tough times ahead.

Goblins and trolls appear in a number of modern trading card games, such as *Magic: The Gathering,* and in video games such as *Warhammer.*

SELECTED BIBLIOGRAPHY

Appenzeller, Tim, et al. *The Enchanted World: Dwarfs.* Alexandria, VA: Time-Life Books, 1985.

Borges, Jorge Luis, and Margarita Guerrero. *The Book of Imaginary Beings.* Translated by Norman Thomas di Giovanni. New York: E. P. Dutton, 1969.

Briggs, Katharine. *An Encyclopedia of Fairies, Hobgoblins, Brownies, Bogies and Other Supernatural Creatures.* New York: Pantheon Books, 1976.

D'Aulaire, Ingrid and Edgar. *D'Aulaire's Trolls.* Garden City, NY: Doubleday, 1972.

Keightley, Thomas. *The World Guide to Gnomes, Fairies, Elves and Other Little People.* New York: Gramercy Books, 2000.

Lunge-Larsen, Lise. *The Hidden Folk: Stories of Fairies, Dwarfs, Selkies and Other Secret Beings.* Boston: Houghton Mifflin, 2004.

Manning-Sanders, Ruth. *A Book of Dwarfs.* New York: E. P. Dutton, 1963.

Manning-Sanders, Ruth. *A Book of Ogres and Trolls.* New York: E. P. Dutton, 1972.

FURTHER READING AND WEBSITES

Black, Holly. *Arthur Spiderwick's Field Guide to the Fantastical World Around You.* Illustrated by Tony DiTerlizzi. New York: Simon & Schuster, 2005. Color plates, black-and-white sketches, and informative text highlight this guide to trolls, brownies, boggarts, pixies, pookas, and other magical creatures.

Briggs, K. M. *Hobberdy Dick.* New York: Greenwillow Books, 1977. Hobberdy Dick is a seventeenth-century hobgoblin who keeps watch over an English manor house. When a Puritan (a strict religious sect) family

moves in, Dick fears that they will drive all the fun from the house. His only hope lies with two of the children, who still love the old ways.

Encyclopedia Mythica. http://www.pantheon.org/. This website contains thousands of articles on myths and mythical creatures from around the world. Search their database for information on the folklore surrounding goblins, gnomes, trolls, and other watchers in the woods.

Folklore and Mythology Electronic Texts. http://www.pitt.edu/~dash/folk-texts.html. This University of Pittsburgh project features stories, tales, myths, fables, and sagas from many countries. The folk texts area features stories categorized by type. Other sections offer archaeological photographs, cultural information, and links to related sites.

Huygen, Will. *Gnomes.* Illustrated by Rien Poortvliet. New York: Harry N. Abrams, Inc., 1977. This is a very thorough examination of the habits and customs of gnomes. Dutch writer Huygen and Dutch artist Poortvliet cover gnome architecture, education, family life, work, and entertainment.

Rowling, J. K. *Harry Potter and the Sorcerer's Stone.* New York: Scholastic, 1998. Readers are introduced to Harry Potter as he discovers his mysterious magical powers and is accepted at the Hogwarts School of Witchcraft and Wizardry. In this book and in the rest of the series, Rowling adds her own touches to watcher lore, creating money-lending goblins, security guard trolls, garden-wrecking gnomes, and shape-shifting boggarts.

Tolkien, J. R. R. *The Hobbit.* 1937. Reprint, Boston: Houghton Mifflin, 2002. A humble hobbit named Bilbo Baggins is enlisted by a troop of dwarfs to help them retrieve a great treasure from the clutches of an evil dragon. The story continues in the follow-up novels, known as the *Lord of the Rings* trilogy.

MOVIES

Gremlins. Burbank, CA: Warner Home Video, 2002. In this classic 1984 movie, a teenager fails to follow the rules in taking care of his mysterious new pet. As a result, the boy's quiet hometown is overrun by a horde of nasty, destructive gremlins. The DVD edition includes commentary by the director and cast and a behind-the-scenes documentary.

Harry Potter and the Sorcerer's Stone. Burbank, CA: Warner Home Video, 2002, DVD. Leaving behind an unhappy home life, Harry journeys to Hogwarts School of Witchcraft and Wizardry. At the school, he meets his share of watchers, including goblins, trolls, and elves. Other Harry Potter movies include *The Chamber of Secrets* (2003 DVD), *The Prisoner of Azkaban* (2004 DVD), and *The Goblet of Fire* (2006 DVD).

Labyrinth. Culver City, CA: Columbia TriStar Home Video, 2000, DVD. Superb special effects highlight this 1986 movie about a teenage girl trying to rescue her little brother, who has been kidnapped by the goblin king.

The Lord of the Rings: The Motion Picture Trilogy. New York: New Line Home Video, 2003. Hobbits, elves, dwarfs, trolls, and goblins inhabit the lavish movie versions of Tolkien's epic battle between good and evil in Middle Earth. The boxed DVD set includes extended editions of *The Fellowship of the Ring*, *The Two Towers*, and *The Return of the King*. Special features include interviews with cast members, documentaries on costumes and art design, behind-the-scenes photographs, and information on J. R. R. Tolkien.

INDEX

ABOUT THE AUTHOR

Stephen Krensky is the author of many fiction and nonfiction books for children, including titles in the On My Own Folklore series and *Bigfoot*, *The Bogeyman*, *Dragons*, *Frankenstein*, *Ghosts*, *The Mummy*, *Vampires*, *Watchers in the Woods*, *Werewolves*, and *Zombies*. When he isn't hunched over his computer, he makes school visits and teaches writing workshops. In his free time, he enjoys playing tennis and softball and reading books by other people. Krensky lives in Massachusetts with his wife, Joan, and their family.

PHOTO ACKNOWLEDGMENTS

The images in this book are used with permission of: © George Ostertag/SuperStock, pp. 2–3; © age fotostock/SuperStock, pp. 8, 22 (background); Erich Lessing/Art Resource, NY, p. 9; © Mary Evans Picture Library/The Image Works, pp. 10, 13, 30, 31; Mary Evans Picture Library/Everett Collection, pp. 16, 20, 28; © Archivo Iconografico, S.A./CORBIS, p. 18; © Topham/The Image Works, pp. 19, 23; Gnomes © Wil Huygen and Rien Poortvliet, 1977. Published by Harry N. Abrams, Inc., New York. All Rights Reserved, p. 22; The Granger Collection, New York, p. 26; © Getty Images, p. 27; © Time & Life Pictures/Getty Images, p. 32; George Macdonald, *The Princess and the Goblin*, Blackie, London, n.d., p. 36; © Disney Enterprises, Inc. Image provided by Everett Collection, p. 39; © 2007 The Jim Henson Company. LABYRINTH is a trademark of The Jim Henson Company. Labyrinth characters © 1986 Labyrinth Enterprises. All Rights Reserved. Photo provided courtesy of The Jim Henson Company, p. 40; "The Lord of the Rings: The Fellowship of the Ring" Copyright MMI, New Line Productions, Inc. TM The Saul Zaentz Company d/b/a Tolkien Enterprises under license to New Line Productions, Inc. All rights reserved. Photo by Pierre Vinet. Photo appears courtesy of New Line Productions, Inc., p. 41; "SPIDER-MAN" Motion Picture © 2002 Columbia Pictures Industries, Inc. All Rights Reserved. Spider-Man Character™ & © 2007 Marvel Characters, Inc. All Rights Reserved. Courtesy of Columbia Pictures. Image provided by Everett Collection, p. 42; © Melvin Levine/Time & Life Pictures/Getty Images, p. 43; Illustrations by © Bill Hauser/Independent Picture Service, pp. 1, 6–7, 14–15, 24–25, 34–35. All page backgrounds illustrated by © Bill Hauser/Independent Picture Service.

Cover illustration by © Bill Hauser/Independent Picture Service.